Waste-free Lunches

by Janine Scott

T0363283

OXFORD
UNIVERSITY PRESS
AUSTRALIA & NEW ZEALAND

Waste-wise Schools

Today, many schools are waste-wise.
Some have waste-free lunch days.
The aim is to reduce the amount of rubbish
and have **zero waste** at lunchtime.
Students must not throw away plastic straws,
juice cartons, packets or food scraps.

Monitors collect food scraps
for the compost bin.

On waste-free days, students only bring items that can be eaten, reused or recycled.

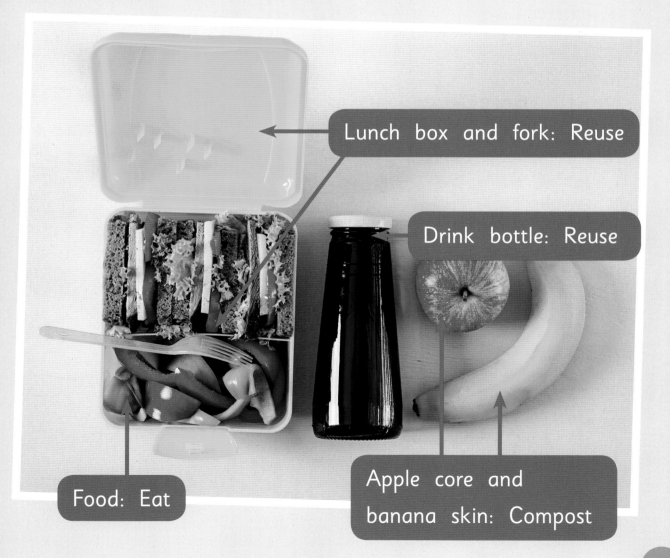

Lunch box and fork: Reuse

Drink bottle: Reuse

Apple core and banana skin: Compost

Food: Eat

No Packets, Please!

Supermarkets are full of food in **packaging**.

Sultanas come in cardboard boxes.

Chips come in foil bags.

Muesli bars come in plastic wrappers.

A washable cloth napkin can be used to wrap up food.

For a waste-free lunch, you put your food straight into your lunch box.

You do not use paper, plastic wrap or foil to wrap it.

You do not bring foods that are already in packaging.

Food that has no packaging is often called Nude Food.

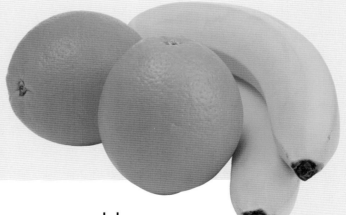

Fruits such as oranges and bananas have their own natural wrapping!

Buying in Bulk

Try not to buy food and drinks in individual packets. Instead, buy food in bulk. It helps to reduce waste.

You can buy food from bulk-bin shops.
The food there has no plastic or cardboard packaging.
Take your own containers to fill up in the shop.

At a bulk-bin shop you can buy as little or as much as you like.

For example, you could fill a large container with sultanas to buy.
Take out enough sultanas for your lunch.
Then, put the sultanas into your lunch box.

Bulk-bin shops sell liquid and solid foods.

A Reusable Lunch Box

What do you pack your food in for a waste-free lunch?

You can use a reusable lunch box!

You can take it to school and bring it home to wash and use again.

This lunchbox has different **compartments** for different foods.

Compartment

Remember to bring reusable drink containers, too.

A metal spoon or fork is washable and reusable.

9

Food In, Compost Out

'R' is for reuse, reduce and recycle.
It is also for **rot**.
Many schools collect food scraps
at the end of lunchtime.
Food monitors put the scraps
in a compost bin or a worm farm.
There, the food waste rots
and turns into compost
for the garden.

Chop up the food scraps
so the worms can eat them easily.

Avoid putting in meat, bones and dairy products.

Paper and garden waste can be added to the food waste.

For a worm farm, you need hundreds of special worms.

They eat the food waste and turn it into castings.

These are good for the garden.

Recycle It!

After reducing, reusing and rotting, recycling is the last option.
Some food packaging can be recycled.
Yoghurt containers and cardboard boxes can be recycled.
This means that it will be collected and made into something else.

Plastic bottles are broken down into tiny pieces and used to make new things.

Recycled plastic can be used to make bottles, playgrounds and even shoes!

This playground is made from recycled plastic.

Being Waste-free

Waste-wise schools reduce, reuse, rot and recycle.

They reduce waste, and they reuse and recycle as many things as they can.

They aim for zero waste.

Waste-free lunch days are a great way for schools to reduce, reuse and recycle.

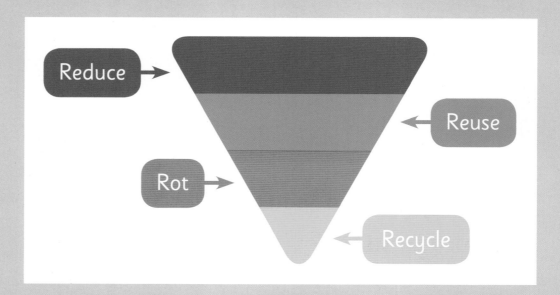

Glossary

compartments	sections
monitors	students who have a special job in the classroom
packaging	wrapping that is around something
rot	to break down or decay
zero waste	no rubbish at all

Index